155 Harry

Potter Facts

THE ULTIMATE

TRIVIA BOOK FOR

WIZARDS AND

WITCHES

of this publication is strictly prohibited and any storage of this document is not allowed unless with written permission from the publisher. All rights reserved.

The information provided herein is stated to be truthful and consistent, in that any liability, in terms of inattention or otherwise, by any usage or abuse of any policies, processes, or directions contained within is the solitary and utter responsibility of the recipient reader. Under no circumstances will any legal responsibility or blame be held against the publisher for any reparation, damages, or monetary loss due to the information herein, either directly or indirectly.

Respective authors and companies own all copyrights not held by the publisher.

The information herein is offered for informational purposes solely and is universal as so. The presentation of the information is without a contract or any type of guarantee assurance.

The trademarks that are used are without any consent, and the publication of the trademark is without permission or backing by the trademark owner. All trademarks and brands within this book are for clarifying purposes only and are owned by the owners themselves, not affiliated with this document.

1. Ageing Potion vs Dumbledore's Age Line

In the Goblet of Fire, Fred and George Weasley attempt to manipulate their ages by drinking an Ageing Potion so they can enter into the Triwizard Tournament. Dumbledore's spell, however, is strong enough to detect the potion thus failing the boys' attempt into beating the system.

2. Voldemort's Inability to Love

Since Voldemort's father was under the effects of a Love Potion when Voldemort was born, the Dark Lord is unable to feel any love. Any child born while one of their parent is under the effects of a Love Potion will be unable to feel any love since the love of one of the parents is forced.

3.   Boggarts

Boggarts are shape-shifting creates that take the form of whatever is scariest to the person in front of them. In other words, they take shape of your worst fear. The more fearful you are as a person, the more susceptible you are to Boggarts since they are attracted to fear.

4. Voldemort's Greatest Fear and his Boggart's Form

Voldemort's greatest fear is his own death which is why he created so many Horcruxes. Therefore, if a Boggart were to appear in front of him, it would take the form of Voldemort's corpse. This has been confirmed by J.K. Rowling.

5. I open at the close

This phrase appears on the golden snitch that Dumbledore passes on to Harry. It comes from the fact that the Harry Potter and the Philosopher's Stone (the first book in the series) was published in 1998 which is the year the Battle of Hogwarts, the final battle in the series, took place.

6.   Professor Trelawney's Curse

A Seer is someone who is able to see into the future through supernatural means. Professor Trelawney's great great grandmother was a pure Seer but her gift was diluted over the generations and was not as strong in her great great granddaughter. In Greek mythology, a Seer named Cassandra was put under a curse which made no one believe in her prophecies. Similarly in the series, no one believed Professor Trelawney's prophecies.

7. The Mirror of Erised

The Mirror shows a person their strongest wishes. When Harry stands in front of the Mirror, he sees his family alive and reunited. Dumbledore sees the same thing as Harry since his family was also torn apart. Erised is simply desire spelled backwards.

8. Went Down Laughing

Sirius Black and Fred Weasley were both infamous pranksters in their days at Hogwarts and both died laughing even as they were taken down.

9. Dudley's Magical Child

J.K. Rowling has said that she almost wrote Dudley, Harry's Muggle cousin, into the epilogue, standing at Platform 9 ¾ with a magical child. She changed her mind however, mentioning that "any latent wizarding genes would never survive contact with Uncle Vernon's DNA."

10. The Patronus Prediction

Ron's Patronus is a Jack Russell terrier while Hermione's is an otter. Jack Russell terriers are known to chase otters. This is most likely a foreshadowing of Ron eventually marrying Hermione.

11. No More Patronus Charms

After his twin brother Fred's death, George Weasley was unable to summon a Patronus ever again. Since Patronus charms require a wizard to conjure up their happiest memories in order to give it power, it is likely that George had gone into depression meaning he could not feel enough happy emotions to cast the charm.

12. Headmaster Snape's Portrait

Since Snape had abandoned his post as Headmaster of Hogwarts, his portrait was not hung in the Headmaster's Office. Harry, however, changed that and had it hung to honor Snape's sacrifice and dedication to defeating Voldemort.

13. Leaving the Same Way I Came In

Harry Potter was dropped off as a baby to 4 Privet Drive, the home of his Aunt Petunia and Uncle Vernon, by Hagrid on Sirius Black's motorcycle. At the end of the series, he leaves in the same motorcycle with Hagrid.

14. What Could Have Been

According to Rowling, Lily Potter (then Lily Evans) could have fallen in love with Snape if he had not chosen to pursue the Dark Arts. However, this potentially means we would have had a Harry Snape instead of a Harry Potter!

15. Gandalf the Grey

In Harry Potter and the Chamber of Secrets, a picture of Gandalf the Grey from Lord of the Rings can be seen in a Collection of Great Wizards book in Dumbledore's study. This is a tribute to Gandalf who is considered one of the most iconic wizards in modern literature.

16. Dumbledore's Crush

Dumbledore, one of the most powerful wizards of all time, was gay as revealed by J.K. Rowling. He had a crush on Grindelwald who he grew up with as a teenage boy. However, it is unclear whether Grindelwald shared the same feelings toward Dumbledore.

17. Finish Your Homework, Kids!

During the scenes in which Harry, Ron and Hermione can be seen doing schoolwork, they were actually doing their own real homework from school. That goes to show that even child actors in the biggest movies still have to finish their homework!

18. You're an Actor, Hagrid!

Robbie Coltrane who plays Rubeus Hagrid in the films was the first actor to be cast. This is most likely because of the size requirement needed to play the character which narrowed down the number of actors who could actually play him.

19. The 7 Hedwigs

A total of 7 owls played the role of Hedwig in the films with 3 being in the first film alone. The names of these owls are Gizmo, Kasper, Oops, Swoops, Oh Oh, Elmo, and Bandit.

20. Harry's Scar

In the books, Harry's scar is in the middle of his forehead while in the films, it is more off to the side. Rowling specifically requested this to be changed for the film adaptation most likely to make it more of a subtle detail.

21. Float Like a Butterfly, Sting Like a Bumblebee?

Dumbledore in Old English means bumblebee. Rowling said it brought her joy to imagine Albus wandering around the castle humming like a bee.

22. Moaning Myrtle's Real Age

The actress who portrayed Moaning Myrtle was actually 37 years old and was the oldest actor/actress to portray a Hogwarts student (both past and present) in the series.

23. If J.K. Rowling were in the Wizarding World

When asked what she would teach if she were a professor at Hogwarts, Rowling said she instruct Charms class. If she had to choose a specific job, she would be an author of spell books, which makes sense since she is an author!

24. Symbols of Depression

Dementors were created based on Rowling's own battles with depression. She explained depression as a "cold absence of feeling – that really hollowed out feeling. That's what Dementors are." This also explains why they can be expelled by Patronus charms. If depression is the absence of happy feeling then being struck by intense happiness is the counter.

25. Hermione's Buck Teeth

Emma Watson originally had to wear buck teeth in the film to make her look like how she was described in the books. However, she could not talk properly with them on so they were taken out.

26. Alan Rickman the Master of Secrets

To help him prepare for his role as Severus Snape, Rowling revealed many spoilers to Alan. Many of these were not told to anyone else until the final book was published.

27. The Many Uses of Dragon Blood

Albus Dumbledore wrote about the 12 Uses of Dragon Blood but the only ones revealed to us are that it is a surprisingly effective oven cleaner and spot remover.

28. Back on the New York Bestseller List

The Harry Potter books were the first children's books to make the list since Charlotte's Web in 1952.

29. The Craze for Harry Potter

There was so much demand and craze for the series that when Harry Potter and the Prisoner of Azkaban was to be released, the publisher asked that the books not be sold until after schools were closed for the day in order to prevent children from skipping class.

30. Harry's Green Eyes

Similar to Emma Watson's buck teeth failure, Daniel Radcliffe was given green contact lenses to match his appearance in the books, but he had an allergic reaction to the lenses. They cancelled the green eyes and proceeded.

31. Lily Potter = J.K. Rowling?

Rowling was offered the role of Lily Potter but she rejected it and it was given to Geraldine Somerville instead.

32. Not Spiders!

Rupert Grint who plays Ron Weasley actually has a terrible fear of spiders so in all the scenes with spiders in the Chamber of Secrets, the fear you see is genuine.

33. Real Food in the Great Hall

In the first movie, all the food in the Great Hall is actually real. However, due to the bright lights and heat, it spoiled quickly which forced the filmmakers to use fake food later on.

34. The Black Family Portrait

The Black family portrait in the Order of the Phoenix, which shows the generations of the Black family, is authentic. Rowling provided over 70 names for the tapestry as well as their relations to each other.

35. Dolores Umbridge, the Maser of Pink

Tonk's hair is supposed to be pink according to the books, but it was made purple since pink was so heavily associated with Umbridge. Who knew pink could be so evil?

36.   The Importance of Colour

Throughout the series, two common colors shown are red and green. Red is typically linked to good while green is linked more with evil. Some examples of this include House Gryffindor being red and shown as a the protagonist house while Slytherin is shown more as an antagonist house. Additionally, Avada Kedavra, the Killing Curse, is green in colour while Expelliarmus, the Disarming Curse, is red in colour.

37.   Harry Potter's Birthday

Harry Potter shares the same birthday as J.K. Rowling – July 31. The years are obviously different however with Harry being born in 1980 and Rowling in 1966.

38. J.K. Rowling of Hufflepuff

When she took an Sorting Hat quiz online, she was placed into Hufflepuff.

39. Here Comes the Money

Rowling is the first person to become a billionaire by writing books.

40. Representation of the Patronus Charm

Similar to how the physical manifestation of their Patronus charms foreshadowed Hermione and Ron being together later on, James and Lily Potter shared something similar. James's Patronus is a stag while Lily's is a doe. Furthermore, Snape's Patronus is also a doe which symbolizes his love for Lily.

41. Hogwarts is a Bunch of Abandoned Ruins

Many charms are cast on Hogwarts caste to prevent it from being stumbled upon by

Muggles. One of these include making Hogwarts appear to be a bunch of old ruins included with a "Keep Out: Dangerous" sign.

42. Ouch That Had to Hurt!

When Fred and George charmed snowballs to hit Professor Quirrel, they unknowingly were striking Voldemort in the face. Ouch!

43. Harry and Ron's Crush

Both Rupert Grint and Daniel Radcliffe admitted to having a crush on Emma Watson in the earlier films.

44. Draco as Harry or Ron?

Tom Felton, who played Draco Malfoy in the films, originally auditioned for Harry and Ron but was given the role of Malfoy. Thank goodness for that!

45. All the Plants are Real

All the plants found in the Wizarding World are actually real. Rowling used all the plants that sounded "witchy" from Culpeper's Complete Herbal by 17th century botanist and herbalist Nicholas Culpeper. However, that doesn't mean you will be able to easily find them in your local grocery store!

46. Harry Potter and the School of Magic

That was the proposed title for the North American release of the film but was rejected by Rowling. Instead, it was called Harry Potter and the Sorcerer's Stone.

47. Top Secret

In order to prevent early leaks of the Deathly Hallows, the publisher had to give it codenames. These included Edinburgh Potmakers and The Life and Times of Clara Rose Lovett: An Epic Novel Covering Many Generations. Much less interesting to say the least!

48. Hagrid the Immortal

Rowling revealed that Hagrid was never in any dangers throughout the writing of the books. This is because she pictured one of the last scenes in the books as Hagrid carrying Harry back from the Forbidden Forest and into Hogwarts. She wanted Hagrid to do it since he was the one to bring Harry into the Wizarding World.

49. Harry and Hermione Together Forever?

J.K. Rowling admits regret for having Ron and Hermione end up together and feels Harry and Hermione would have made a much better match.

50. Born for Greatness

Dumbledore's full name is Albus Wulfric Percival Brian Dumbledore. Albus means white in Latin which represents good and light. Wulfric was a saint in the ancient times further representing the idea of good and the light. Percival was one of the famed knights at King Arthur's Round Table. Brian is a Celtic name meaning strong.

51. Meaning of Voldemort

Voldemort is based off French words which translate to "flight of death". This further strengthens his need for immortality and escaping death.

52. The Prisoner of Azkaban

Although it was never told in the books of what happened to Dolores Umbridge, it was confirmed by Rowling that she was imprisoned in Azkaban. Hopefully all that pink doesn't attract too many Dementors!

53. Another Orphan

Lupin and Tonks were not originally intended to be killed but Rowling changed her mind so that another orphan could be created. This was done in order to further showcase the damage and pain brought about by Voldemort.

54. Keeping the Bloodline Pure

Fiennes-Tiffin, the actor who plays the young Tom Riddle in the orphanage, is the nephew of Ralph Fiennes who plays the Voldemort we all know and love/hate.

55. Bill Weasley the Son of Mad-Eye Moody

Doomhall Gleeson who plays Bill Weasley is the son of Brendan Gleeson who plays Mad-Eye Moody.

56. So Many Glasses, So Little Time

Radcliffe went through 160 pairs of glasses by the time the series was finished. If only Reparo could be used in real life!

57. Harry Potter and the Doomspell Tournament

The Goblet of Fire was going to be called Harry Potter and the Doomspell Tournament. Thank goodness Rowling changed her mind!

58. No Leaks!

The publishers of Harry Potter spend millions on trying to make sure the Harry Potter books were not leaked before release. However despite all the effort and capital, there were still numerous leaks on multiple illegal pirating sites.

59. Hello, Bonjour, Ni Hao, and Hola

Harry Potter has been translated in over 70 languages making it one of the most translated books in history.

60. Origins of Muggle

"Muggle" as a word actually existed in the 1950s and was used to describe people who smoked cannabis.

61. The Shortest Film

Harry Potter and the Deathly Hallows Part 2 is the shortest film in the series at 2 hours and 10 minutes.

62. The Longest Film

Harry Potter and the Chamber of Secrets is the longest film in the series at 2 hours and 54 minutes.

63. Hedwig the Saint of Owls

Hedwig shares her name with two famous saints: Saint Hedwig of Andechs and Saint Hedwig, Queen of Poland. Both were noted for being compassionate and kind. It is interesting to note that Hedwig's death represents a sort of loss of innocence for Harry.

64.   Harry Potter the Drummer

Daniel Radcliffe broke approximately 80 wands during the filming of the series because he would use the wands as drumsticks.

65.   British Only

Rowling insisted on having the entire cast be from Britain only. In fact, she turned down even Robin Williams and Rosie O'Donnell despite their offer to work without pay.

66.   Rowling's Favorite Actor?

Alan Rickman, the actor who played Snape, was handpicked by Rowling herself to play

Snape. Perhaps he was the only one she trusted with the secrets?

67. Emma Watson's Audition

Watson initially did not want to audition for the role of Hermione when the casting team was auditioning her school. Her teacher, however, gave her encouragement to audition and the rest is history. She was the last girl to audition for her school that day.

68. Rowling's Favorite Mythical Beast

Her favourite beast is the Phoenix, which is a mythical bird that is reborn every 500 to 1000 years from its own ashes. A Phoenix saved

Harry during his battle with the Basilisk in the Chamber of Secrets.

69. Is Rowling a Believer in Magic?

Despite being a huge fan of magic herself, she does not actually believe in it at all.

70. Ernie and Stanley

The driver and conductor of the Knight Bus, Ernie and Stanley, are named after Rowling's grandfathers.

71. Hogwarts or Hogworts?

Rowling said she may have chosen the name of Hogwarts School based on a hogwort plant she saw in the Kew Gardens in New York City.

72. If J.K. Rowling Drank Polyjuice Potion

If she were to drink the potion, she would transform into former Prime Minister Tony Blair. Getting a piece of his hair may turn out to be difficult however.

73. Rowling's Favourite Animal

Rowling's favourite animal is an otter. This is the reason Hermione's Patronus takes the shape of an otter because Rowling sees many similarities between herself and Hermione.

74. Abhadda kedhabhra?

Avada Kedavra, the Killing Curse, comes from the Aramaic word Abhadda kedhabhra which means "to disappear like this word". It may also come from Abracadabra. Both of these words were used to cure illnesses in ancient times.

75. Sirius Black's Tattoos

Sirius's tattoos are inspired by Russian prison gangs. They identify someone who is to be feared and respected. This makes sense since Sirius Black was a powerful wizard and both respected and feared.

76. The Philosopher's Stone

The Philosopher's Stone is an ancient relic or substance that was believed to turn ordinary metals into gold. It was sought after by many alchemists in old times but so far it remains a myth.

77. The Knights of Walpurgis

This is what the Death Eaters were originally to be known as. The name is based on Walpurgis Night which is a old witch's holiday on April 30th during which demons and witches were free to roam the land.

78. Morsmorde

Morsmorde is the spell used to make the Death Mark appear in the sky. It translates to "take a bite out of death" in French which is quite fitting for the Death "Eaters".

79. The Essays

The Prisoner of Azkaban's director asked Emma, Daniel, and Rupert, each to write essays from the point of view of their characters. True to their characters, Emma wrote a 10 page essay, Daniel wrote 1 page, and Rupert wrote nothing at all.

80. The Hogwarts School Motto

The Hogwarts motto is *Draco Dormiens Nunquam Titillandus* which means "Never Tickle a Sleeping Dragon". Harry clearly did not take this motto to heart throughout his adventures in the series.

81. The Location of Hogwarts

Hogwarts is located somewhere in Scotland.

82. How Old is Hogwarts?

Hogwarts is approximately 1000 years old and was founded by Godric Gryffindor, Salazar Slytherin, Helga Hufflepuff, and Rowena Ravenclaw.

83. Grading System of Hogwarts

In Hogwarts, grades are not given out as percentages or letters. The passing grades are Outstanding, Exceeds Expectations, and

Acceptable. The failing grades are Poor, Dreadful, and Troll.

84. How Did Harry Potter Come About?

While stuck at a 4 hour train delay, Rowling said that the idea simply "strolled into her head".

85. Rowling's Favourite Book as a Child

Her favourite book when she was young was The Little White Horse by Elizabeth Goudge.

86.   Lice Outbreak, Run!

During the filming of the Chamber of Secrets, there was an outbreak of lice amongst the child actors.

87.   The Masters of Death

Dumbledore and Harry are the only two known wizards who have been in possession of all 3 Deathly Hallows at one time, effectively making them the masters of death according to legend.

88. Getting to the Ministry of Magic

A secret code must be dialled into a telephone keypad in order to gain access as shown by Arthur Weasley when he takes Harry and his friends. The number he enters is 62442 which happens to spell out "magic".

89. A Fitting Birthday

Fred and George Weasley celebrate their birthdays on April Fools which is fitting for two of the most infamous pranksters in the series.

90. Sirius, the Dog Star

Sirius Black is named after this star which is the brightest star in the sky. This is also why his Animagus shape is in the form of a dog.

91. End of a Reign of Terror

In 1945, both the Muggle World and Wizarding World defeated the biggest tyrants at the time: Adolf Hitler and Gellert Grindelwald.

92. Wizarding Currency

29 bronze knuts make a silver sickle and 17 silver sickles make a gold galleon.

93. Dolores Umbridge, the Evilest Witch in the World

Rowling revealed that Dolores Umbridge is as evil as Voldemort. I don't think that pink is work

94. Hatstalls

A hatstall is referred to when the Sorting Hat is unable to choose a House for a student for over 5 minutes.

95. Uncle Voldemort

Voldemort and Harry Potter are related through their connection to the Peverell family. The Cloak of Invisibility was passed down from Ignotus Peverell to the Potter family while the Resurrection Stone was passed down to the Gaunt family by Cadmus Peverell.

96. Voldemort the Half Blood Prince

Voldemort is not actually a pure blooded wizard though he boasts about them to the highest ends. His father, Tom Riddle, was a Muggle.

97. The Rise of Hufflepuff

Hufflepuff won the House Cup in 2015 which is a change of pace from the usual pride of being either Slytherin or Griffindor. Cedric

Diggory and Newt Scamander are also notable figures from Hufflepuff.

98. October 31st, 1991

This special date marks the day that Hermione, Ron, and Harry defeated the troll in the girls' bathroom and is accepted as the official day that the trio became friends. It is also the 10th year death anniversary of Harry's parents and the day that Voldemort was defeated.

99. Nicholas Flamel, the Philosopher

Nicholas Flamel was a real alchemist who made it his life's mission to produce the Philosopher's Stone.

100. First Day of School at Hogwarts

The term for Hogwarts begins on September 1st.

101. Newt Scamander in Prisoner of Azkaban

Newt's name can be found on the Marauder's Map in the Prisoner of Azkaban.

102. Newt = Tom Riddle?

Eddie Redmayne, the actor who plays Newt Scamander, in Fantastic Beasts and Where to Find Them, originally auditioned to play Tom Riddle in the Chamber of Secrets but was turned down after saying just one line.

103. American Wizard Currency

The currency for wizards in America is called Dragots.

104. Born to be a Master of Beasts

Newt's full name is Newton Artemis Fido Scamander. A newt is a small salamander,

Artemis is the Greek goddess of animals, Fido is a popular dog name, and scamander is very similar to salamander. No wonder he loves animals and beasts so much!

105. Both Lovers of Animals Expelled from Hogwarts

Both Hagrid and Newt, who are two of the iconic animal loving characters, were expelled from Hogwarts.

106. Luna Lovegood and Newt's Relation

Luna Lovegood ends up marrying Newt's grandson, Rolf Scamander and even had two children, Lorcan and Lysander.

107. The Source of Harry's Wealth

How does Harry end up with such a large inheritance of piles of galleons when he visits Gringotts for the first time? Turns out that Harry's ancestor Linfred of Stinchcombe invented medical remedies that formed a basis for Skele-gro and Pepperup Potion and the fortune made from it was maintained for years.

108. Gringotts' Magical Exchange

Gringotts has the ability to convert Muggle money such as pounds and euros into galleons, knuts, and sickles. How do you think Muggle born wizards buy anything in the wizarding world?

109. The Original Harry Potter

Harry's great grandfather's name was Henry Potter but his close friends and family referred to him as Harry.

110. Dumbledore the Transfiguration Professo

Before he was Headmaster, Dumbledore was a transfiguration teacher. This was his position when he met both Newt Scamander and Tom Riddle, who were both his students.

111. Just Another Trashy Airport Novel

Rita Skeeter's "The Life and Lies of Dumbledore" was intentionally made to look like a poor-quality book by Rowling to emphasize how little credibility it had.

112. Latin the not so Dead Language

Most of the spells in Harry Potter are based on Latin. For example, Accio, which summons an object to you, comes from the word accerso which means to summon or to fetch.

113. The Missing Prequel

Rowling wrote a short story about James Potter and Sirius Black which is about them fooling around on magical motorbikes and running from Muggle police. She auctioned the handwritten draft in 2008. However, the handwritten draft was stolen in April 2017 and still has not been found.

114. The Magical Portraits

Many of the magical portraits in Hogwarts are of the producers themselves. They wanted to immortalize themselves in some way through the movie.

115. The Only Graduate

Hermione is the only member of the trio to complete her academics at Hogwarts. Ron and Harry went straight for auror training and did not complete their 7th years.

116. The Resurrection Stone

The Resurrection Stone has still not been found after being pressed into the ground by centaurs.

117. Draco's Initial Reaction to Harry

Remember when Draco was actually nice to Harry when he first met him? Turns out that Lucius Malfoy, Draco's father, hoped that Harry would be a powerful dark wizard and raised his son with that optimism.

118. No More Parseltongue

When the part of Voldemort inside Harry was destroyed, he also lost his ability to speak Parseltongue.

119. No More Death Eaters

With the exception of the Malfoys, all the Death Eaters were either imprisoned in Azkaban or killed.

120. As Long as the Heart Stays Young

In 2017, Hagrid at 88 years old is still working at Hogwarts.

121. No Animagus for Harry

Unlike his father James whose Animagus form was that of a stag, Harry does not end up training to be an Animagus because "his energies are going to be concentrated elsewhere and he's not going to have time to do that."

122. RIP Order of the Phoenix

The Order was disbanded after the Battle of Hogwarts since Voldemort was defeated.

123. Professor Longbottom

Neville Longbottom becomes Professor of Herbology at Hogwarts after serving as an auror for multiple years.

124. Clearing Snape's Name

Very shortly after defeating Voldemort, Harry made sure to clear Snape's name and honour him as a hero.

125. Viktor Krum

After the Triwizard Tournament, Viktor Krum returned to Bulgaria, finished his schooling, fell in love, and presumably lived happily ever after.

126. American Hogwarts

The American counterpart to Hogwarts is called Ilvermorny School of Witchcraft and Wizardry.

127. The First Werewolf

Remus Lupin was awarded the Order of Merlin, First Class, making him the first werewolf to receive the honour.

128. We Almost Lost Ron

Rowling admits she seriously considered killing Ron at one point when she was in a dark place.

129. Victory Child

Bill and Fleur Weasley's first child was born on the anniversary of the Battle of Hogwarts and was named Victoire which means victory in French.

130. Cho Chang

Cho Chang, who was Harry's crush at one point, married a muggle. After the defeat of

Voldemort, this was beginning to become both more accepted and common.

131. We're Famous!

The Trio each got their own Chocolate Frog cards. Ron claims this to be his life's greatest achievement.

132. Forever in Limbo

Because Voldemort's soul was so corrupted, he is forever stuck in Limbo in the child-like form that Harry saw him in at King's Cross with Dumbledore.

133. Never Give Up

Rowling was rejected by 12 different publishers before one finally agreed to publish Harry Potter. When you fail, don't give up, keep trying.

134. 1000 Years Old

Salazar Slytherin's basilisk, the same one from the Chamber of Secrets, was almost 1000 years old at the time of its death.

135. Scars on Scars on Scars

During the filming of the series, the scar on Daniel Radcliffe's forehead was applied approximately 2000 times.

136. Magical Suitcases

Both Hermione and Newt have enchanted containers which allows them to hold much more than physically possible.

137. Mandatory Reading Material

Newt's book, "Fantastic Beasts and Where to Find Them", is a mandatory textbook for all first year students at Hogwarts.

138. No Electricity or Tech at Hogwarts

Electricity and technology does not work at Hogwarts because magic disrupts it.

139. You're Hired!

Eddie Redmayne did not have to audition for the part of Newt. He was given the part right away by Rowling herself and even allowed to help in other casting decisions. According to producer David Heyman, "Not only does he look as if he lives in 1926, but he has all the elements required to be Newt: he's smart, funny, utterly British, and immensely sympathetic—even as an outsider more comfortable with his beasts than with people."

140. The First Muggle Main Character

Jacob Kowalski from Fantastic Beasts is the first main muggle character in the Harry Potter films.

141. Squibs

A squib is a non magical child born to magical parents.

142. Start off Small

The first printed batch of Harry Potter books contained only 1,000 copies. The rest is history.

143. 500 Million

Today, over 500 million copies of Harry Potter have been sold.

144. Word Invention

Rowling invented the word "choranaptyxic" for the film. A choranaptyxic creature is one that can shrink or grow to fit the available space. The Occamy is an example of this.

145. Closest Town

Hogsmeade is the closest populated town to Hogwarts.

146. A Basilisk's Mortal Weakness

Believe it or not but the mortal weakness of a basilisk is the crow of a rooster. Be sure to have that chicken in your pocket next time you go up against a basilisk!

147. Joanne Rowling

J.K. Rowling's real name is actually Joanne Rowling. She does not have a middle name but she used the 'K' in honour of her grandmother, Kathleen.

148. Rowling Least Favourite Subject

Rowling did not like chemistry growing up which is why she made Snape the Potions professor. However, she found that she actually enjoyed writing about potions.

149. Professor. Rowling

Before becoming one of the most famous authors in history, Rowling was a schoolteacher.

150. The Seven Subjects

The seven required subjects at Hogwarts are Transfiguration, Charms, Potions, History of Magic, Defence Against the Dark Arts, Astronomy, and Herbology.

151. The Book of Admittance

This is an ancient book with a magical quill called the Quill of Acceptance which records the birth of every magical child in the book. This is what is used to admit children into Hogwarts.

152. Keeping it Old School

Rowling completed the first draft of Harry Potter in 1996 on a typewriter.

153. 7 Secret Passages

According to the Marauder's Map, there are a total of 7 secret passages in Hogwarts.

154. Harry Potter the Cartoon

There was once a discussion of making Harry Potter into a series of animated films.

155. Quidditch in Real Life

Quidditch has actually become a real sport in the Muggle world! There are teams in multiple universities and a World Cup but no flying yet unfortunately!

Made in the USA
Columbia, SC
16 November 2019